5 95

D1477972

SHIRLEY STEINBAC

SHAKESPEARE FOR EVERYONE

A MIDSUMMER NIGHT'S DREAM

By Jennifer Mulherin   *Illustrations by* Norman Bancroft-Hunt

Silver Burdett Press · Morristown, New Jersey

Author's note

There is no substitute for seeing the plays of Shakespeare performed. Only then can you really understand why Shakespeare is England's greatest dramatist and poet. This book simply gives you the background to the play and tells you about the story and characters. It will, I hope, encourage you to see the play.

Designed and produced by
A S Publishing

First published 1988
by Cherrytree Press Ltd
a subsidiary of
The Chivers Company Ltd
Windsor Bridge Road
Bath, Avon BA2 3AX

Adapted and first published
in the United States in 1988
by Silver Burdett Press,
Morristown, New Jersey

Copyright © Cherrytree Press Ltd 1988

This adaptation © Silver Burdett Press, 1988

Library of Congress Cataloging-in-Publication Data

Mulherin, Jennifer.
    A midsummer night's dream/Jennifer Mulherin.
       p.   cm. —(Shakespeare for everyone)
    Includes index.
    Summary: Discusses the plot, characters, and historical background
of the Shakespeare play.
    ISBN 0-382-09690-8 (lib. bdg.). ISBN 0-382-09696-7 (pbk.)
    1. Shakespeare, William, 1564-1616. Midsummer night's dream—
Juvenile literature. [1. Shakespeare, William, 1564-1616.
Midsummer night's dream. 2. English literature—History and
criticism.] I. Title. II. Series: Mulherin, Jennifer.
Shakespeare for everyone.
PR2827.M85 1988
822.3'3—dc19

87-37229
CIP
AC

Printed in Hong Kong by Colorcraft Ltd

All rights reserved. No part of this publication may be reproduced, stored in a retrieval system, or transmitted, in any form or by any means without the prior permission in writing of the publisher, nor be otherwise circulated in any form of binding or cover other than that in which it is published and without a similar condition including this condition being imposed on the subsequent purchaser.

Contents

The Life of Shakespeare **3**

Why the Play was Written **9**

The Story of *A Midsummer Night's Dream* **12**

The Play's Characters **26**

Life and Plays of Shakespeare **31**

Index and Acknowledgments **32**

The Life of Shakespeare

R.Greene delin.   B.Cole sculp.ᵗ

A House in Stratford upon Avon, in which the famous Poet Shakespear was Born.

William Shakespeare's birthplace in Henley Street, Stratford-upon-Avon, England. This illustration was made in 1769. The house still exists today and can be visited by the public.

The young Shakespeare

William Shakespeare's family had been humble farmers in Warwickshire, England since the Middle Ages. Then William's father decided to better himself and move to the town of Stratford, only a few miles from the family's home. John Shakespeare set up business as a glove maker, his work prospered and he was soon able to buy two houses in Henley Street, Stratford – and it was in one of these that Shakespeare was born in 1564.

Shakespeare's father had probably known his mother,

Mary Arden, since childhood. Her father owned the land on which the Shakespeare family farmed. The Ardens lived in a large, comfortable house at Wilmcote (near Stratford) and were people of some standing in the district. They were regarded as minor gentry although they were not aristocratic or titled.

William was their third child – the two elder ones had died from plague – and altogether the Shakespeares had eight children. By the time William was old enough to go to school, his father's career had prospered further. He had become an alderman and bailiff (mayor) of the busy market town, and a justice of the peace.

Married at 18 years of age

It is almost certain that William went to the local grammar school where he would have been taught a good deal of Latin and some Greek. He would not have seen many plays in Stratford because in those days there were no public theaters. But strolling players sometimes visited country districts performing pageants. Occasionally miracle plays, in which scenes from the Bible were acted out, were put on in Coventry, only 20 miles away. We do not know what Shakespeare did after he left school but one story says that he became a schoolmaster in the Cotswolds or in Lancashire. What we do know is that at the age of 18 he married Anne Hathaway, the daughter of a Stratford neighbor, who was eight years older than he. In 1853, his daughter Susanna was born and in 1585 the twins Hamnet and Judith. So, by the age of 21, William had not only a wife but three children to support.

Shakespeare becomes an actor in London

Why Shakespeare went to London and when is not certain. Most probably it was to earn some money, although one story relates that it was because he was caught poaching deer and rabbits on Sir Thomas Lucy's estate, Charlecote Park, near Stratford and forced to flee to the city. Whatever the reason, William went to London and became an actor.

From all accounts, Shakespeare was a good actor and he played both comic and tragic parts with different companies of actors. Life in the theater was busy and among other things, William would have learned several actors' parts, because a new play was put on each day. He helped rewrite old plays and at this time was trying his hand at writing plays himself. He toured different areas of the country with the company, he met fellow actors, and played before the nobility and the court. So in a fairly short time, he learned a good deal about life in the city and how it was lived by rich and poor alike – and about the government and the political events of the time.

Shakespeare in love

Unlike many writers at the beginning of their career, Shakespeare was lucky. His work attracted the attention of a young nobleman, the Earl of Southampton, who not only encouraged him to write poetry as well as plays but also introduced him to cultivated people who were interested in art, music, theater, and literature. It was at this time that he met and fell madly in love with the "dark lady" of the *Sonnets* – a dark-haired, married woman who led him on, but in the end broke off their affair. Shakespeare's *Sonnets*, which contain some of the finest poetry written in the English language, express the joy and agony of that relationship.

Shakespeare the playwright

By about 1595 or 1596, Shakespeare was becoming well known as a writer of plays. He had already written some

The Earl of Southampton, Shakespeare's patron. He was a rich, young nobleman of about 20 years of age when Shakespeare met him. Southampton encouraged Shakespeare to write poetry as well as plays.

5

historical plays, including *Richard III*, and also *The Taming of the Shrew* and *Romeo and Juliet*. In 1595, he became a shareholder in one of the most popular acting companies of the day. From then on, he spent the rest of his career writing plays for that company. After 1599 most were performed at the famous Globe Theatre in Southwark, a suburb of London on the south side of the Thames River.

The theatre was one of the most popular kinds of entertainment in those days and Shakespeare wrote his plays for ordinary people. They loved his work and came again and again to see favorites, such as *Richard III* and *Macbeth*. The result was that he made quite a lot of money and was able to buy a large house, New Place, in Stratford. He also bought other property around Stratford. Because his father had been given a coat of arms earlier, Shakespeare was now regarded as a real gentleman and a man of standing – rather like his maternal grandfather.

Shakespeare returns to Stratford

Shakespeare wrote over 35 plays and all of them were performed regularly, although some were more popular than others. In about 1610, Shakespeare left London and returned to Stratford to live; and after 1613 he wrote no more plays. We know almost nothing about his later life in Stratford. His beloved daughter, Susanna, who was married to a doctor, lived nearby and Shakespeare probably just enjoyed his life, living in the company of his family – although it is likely he went to London from time to time.

Shakespeare died in 1616, some say from a fever he developed after a merry evening of eating and drinking with his friends, the poet Michael Drayton and the playwright Ben Jonson. In his will, Shakespeare left most of his possessions to Susanna and her husband and some small gifts to his best friends in the theater company. He left the

Opposite: The town of Stratford-upon-Avon in 1764. Both the church and the stone bridge are still standing. Shakespeare was baptized and buried in the church. And in a niche in the wall of the church, there is a bust of Shakespeare. This was placed there soon after his death.

Theseus's hounds
My love shall hear the music of my hounds.
Uncouple in the western valley, let them go . . .

. . . their heads are hung
With ears that sweep away the morning dew,
Crook-knee'd, and dewlapped like Thessalian bulls;
Slow in pursuit; but matched in mouth like bells.
Each under each. A cry more tuneable
Was never holla'ed to, nor cheered with horn.

Act IV Sci

second best bed to his widow, not as an insult as many people think, but because it was almost certainly the bed they slept in – and because Susanna and her husband, or guests, might need the best one.

Puck's description of game birds

As wild geese that the creeping fowler eye,
Or russet-pated choughs, many in sort,
Rising and cawing at the gun's report
Sever themselves and madly sweep the sky.

Act III Sc ii

Shakespeare's youth and *A Midsummer Night's Dream*

Shakespeare was living in London when he wrote *A Midsummer Night's Dream*. More than any other play, except maybe *As You Like It*, this play draws on his childhood and youth in the countryside around Stratford. The fairy tales and nursery legends heard there were things he carried in his head to London and were not learned from books as the subjects of some of his other plays were – for example, *Macbeth*.

The play is full of all kinds of country activities. Shakespeare must have loved hunting when he was a boy to have written about the hounds and the sound of the birds so well. In another part of the play, Shakespeare talks about morris dancers whom he must have seen often at country fêtes and festivals, and even the tradesmen he describes were like people he would have met in Stratford. In fact, he

A village May Day celebration. Great merrymaking always took place on 1 May in Shakespeare's time.

Ghosts at dawn

*At whose approach, ghosts,
    wandering here and there,
Troop home to churchyards:
    damned spirits all,
That in crossways and floods
    have burial.*
                              Act III Sc iii

Ghosts at night

*Now is the time of night
    That the graves, all gaping
        wide,
Everyone lets forth his sprite,
    In the churchway paths to
        glide.*
                              Act v Sc ii

made a joke of their occupation when he called the weaver Bottom – after the skein (called a "bottom") on which a weaver winds his yarn.

Shakespeare's relatives were farmers, so he knew about work in the dairy and how ordinary village folk lived. The tricks that Puck plays in *A Midsummer Night's Dream* tell us that. And, in Shakespeare's time people believed in ghosts, who came alive at night but returned to their graves at dawn, just as Shakespeare describes.

Perhaps Shakespeare wrote this play because he knew that everyone loves a fairy tale. But it would be nice to think that, although Shakespeare was busy in London and had met all kinds of interesting people, he was sometimes lonely and yearned to be back in Warwickshire with his family and the folks he grew up with – and that he wrote this play in order to remember and recapture some of the joys and experiences of his lost youth in Stratford.

Puck's tricks

*are you not he
That frights the maidens of the
    villagery
Skim milk, and sometimes labour
    in the quern,
And bootless make the breathless
    housewife churn,
And sometimes make the drink to
    bear no barm,
Mislead night-wanderers, laugh-
    ing at their harm?*
                              Act II Sc i

A Play to Celebrate a Wedding?

Country dancing in Elizabethan times. The music is provided by a drum. This illustration comes from a book published when Shakespeare was a young man.

A *Midsummer Night's Dream* begins with the announcement of a wedding and ends with the marriage ceremony for the three couples in the play – Theseus, the Duke of Athens, and his love Hippolyta, and the two sets of young lovers, Hermia and Lysander and Helena and Demetrius. Although no one knows for certain, it is probable that Shakespeare wrote this play to celebrate the marriage of some aristocratic lord and lady with whom he was friendly – and it is most likely that the play was first put on not in a theater but in a private house after the wedding celebrations. Later, of course, it was staged for the general public.

Songs and dances

The play is different in certain ways from most of the other plays Shakespeare was writing around this time (about 1594). It has, for example, quite a few songs and dances in it – which many composers since then have put to music – and which perhaps were accompanied by music at its first performance. Because of this, it is more like the private entertainments, called *masques*, put on before the Queen and her court in those days. These theatrical extravaganzas never told much of a story but created their effect by being beautiful to look at and by using songs, dances, and music to help keep the audience entertained.

What's in a name?

Midsummer night is the night before June 24 and in Shakespeare's day it was always celebrated with festivals, dances, pageants, and general merrymaking. Frequently, the characters in these pageants were fairies, goblins, witches, and devils who could cast spells, change people into birds or animals, and do all kinds of other extraordinary things. So Shakespeare was only following the custom of his time by setting part of the play in a fairy world. Most Elizabethan folk believed in witchcraft and the supernatural. In those days, it was common for people to suffer from midsummer "madness" when, for example, they imagined strange things or behaved in odd ways – as if they were in a trance or a dream, or under a spell cast by fairies.

Sensible people knew that this madness only lasted a very short time and they believed that it was brought on by the long, hot days of summer which, they thought, could weaken a person's mind. So from its title, Shakespeare's audience knew immediately that they would be seeing a play in which there would be fairies and witches to weave spells and in which all sorts of strange things could happen – as they do in a fairy story. And they would have expected to be entertained by songs and dances because, in their local town or village, that was how midsummer night was celebrated.

Above: *Dancing and feasting at a fête. The celebrations were probably in honour of a wedding.*

In an enchanted forest

The play takes place in a forest near the city of Athens in Greece. It is highly unlikely that Shakespeare ever went to Athens himself but like many children who went to grammar school in his day he learned Greek and Roman history. Theseus was a Greek ruler in ancient times and had married a lady called Hippolyta. Chaucer told the story of their meeting in *The Canterbury Tales* and Shakespeare may have borrowed the idea of his play from there, as well as remembering it from his schooldays.

When the play is put on the stage, the actors are often dressed in the kinds of costumes worn by the ancient Greeks – but the setting of the play is really more English than Greek. The fairies, for example, are not much like the gods and spirits found in Greek myths and legends. They are more like those in old English folk stories. And Shakespeare would have heard many folk tales and rhymes when growing up in the Warwickshire countryside. The trees, plants, and animals found in the woods where the fairies live are also found in many parts of the English countryside.

Shakespeare's poetry

People say that this is one of the most "poetic" of Shakespeare's plays. By that they mean that it is full of beautiful sounds and rhythms – so that, even when you do not understand all that Shakespeare is saying, you can still hear the music in the lines and speeches. Some of his descriptions of the natural world, and the people, and the events in the play are also very lovely. He uses words and phrases that stay in our minds. So when we listen to the play, we should be carried along by its wonderful poetry and music into an imaginary world – or a dream – which, as Shakespeare says, is "rich and strange".

11

The Story of A Midsummer Night's Dream

A royal wedding

In Athens, Theseus, Duke of the city, and Hippolyta his love, are to be married in four days' time on the night of the new moon on May 1. While they are discussing their plans, one of the Duke's citizens, Egeus, comes to him with a complaint. Hermia, his daughter has refused to marry Demetrius, a young man her father approves of, because she is in love with someone else.

Lovers' difficulties

The object of her affection is Lysander who, Egeus says, has won her over with compliments and gifts and made her disobedient to her father. The Duke points out that it is against the law in Athens to go against a father's wishes. He explains to Hermia that if she refuses to marry Demetrius, she will either be condemned to death or will have to spend the rest of her life as a nun in a convent – and he gives her the four days until his wedding night to decide what she is going to do.

A plan to run away

As soon as Hermia and Lysander are alone together, he consoles her by telling her that "the course of true love never did run smooth". He thinks up a plan which will allow them to marry but it means running away to his aunt's house – some distance from Athens. Because of different laws in that part of the country, they can marry without Egeus's

permission. The young lovers arrange to meet the next night in a forest near Athens and make their escape from there.

> **Describing Hermia**
> *Your eyes are lode-stars; and your tongue's sweet air*
> *More tuneable than lark to shepherd's ear,*
> *When wheat is green, when hawthorn buds appear .*
>
> Act I Sc i

How Helena betrays her friend

They tell their plan to Helena, Hermia's best friend from her schooldays. Helena has always been in love with Demetrius and at one time he, too, was in love with her. She is unhappy and love-sick and she decides to tell Demetrius of the lovers' plan because, she thinks, he might then be kind and grateful to her. She knows that Demetrius will follow Hermia and Lysander to the woods, so she decides to follow him.

The tradesmen and their play

Meanwhile, all over Athens, events are being planned to celebrate the Duke's wedding. Among the ordinary folk of Athens, some tradesmen have arranged to put on a play for the Duke and his bride. The actors, who are all friends, are Quince, a carpenter, Snug, a joiner, Bottom, a weaver, Flute, a bellows mender, Snout, a tinker, and Starveling, a tailor. These fellows do not know much about writing or acting in plays. They have decided to write a play about the tragedy of two young lovers, Pyramus and Thisbe, but they cannot quite agree about who should play the different parts. So they arrange to meet by moonlight on the following night in a forest outside the town to go through the play without interruption.

Quarrel of Titania and Oberon

Now it is in this same forest outside Athens that Oberon and Titania, the king and queen of the fairies, are to be found. They have come to Athens with their courtiers and attendants to honor the wedding of Theseus and Hippolyta. A mischievous goblin, Puck, is one of Oberon's attendants and we learn from him that Oberon and Titania have had a quarrel over a young Indian boy whom Titania has taken into her service but whom Oberon wants as his pageboy. Titania refuses to give the boy to her husband, so Oberon

decides to play a trick on her. He sends Puck to find a magic flower whose juices can cast a spell over the person into whose eyes it is dropped. When the person wakes up, they fall in love with the first thing they see, whether it is an animal or a human being.

The love potion

While Oberon is hatching his plot, Demetrius comes into the forest in search of Hermia and Lysander – for it is now the following night when the lovers intend to escape. He is angry because he is followed by the forlorn Helena who will not leave him alone, even though he keeps telling her that he does not love her. Oberon, who has overheard their

Where Titania sleeps
I know a bank whereon the wild thyme blows,
Where oxlips and the nodding violet grows
Quite over-canopied with luscious woodbine,
With sweet musk-roses, and with eglantine:
There sleeps Titania some time of the night,
Lull'd in these flowers with dances and delight;

Act II Sci

conversation, feels sorry for Helena – and he decides that, as well as using the magic flower on Titania, he will also make Demetrius fall in love with Helena.

When Puck returns with the flower, Oberon takes some of it to put on Titania's eyes, while she sleeps nearby on a grassy bank. And he sends Puck to use it on Demetrius – who, Oberon tells him, is recognizable by his Athenian clothes. Oberon finds Titania being sung to sleep by her fairies. When they leave her to sleep peacefully in her fairy bower, he squeezes the juices onto her eyelids.

Puck's mistake

In the meantime, Hermia and Lysander have lost their way in the forest. They are weary and exhausted and decide to go to sleep for a little while – lying apart from each other out of modesty because they are not yet married. Moments after they have fallen asleep, Puck finds them and thinking that the young man in Athenian clothes must be Demetrius squeezes the juices into his eyes.

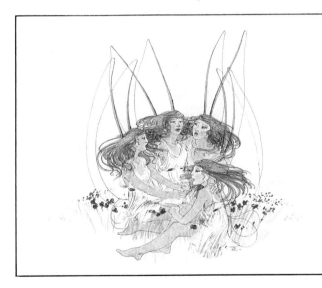

The fairies' song
You spotted snakes with double tongue,
*   Thorny hedge-hogs, be not seen;*
Newts and blind-worms, do no wrong:
*   Come not near our fairy queen.*
*   Philomel, with melody,*
*   Sing in our sweet lullaby;*
Lulla, lulla, lullaby; lulla, lulla, lullaby:
*   Never harm,*
*   Nor spell, nor charm,*
*   Come our lovely lady nigh,*
*   So, good night, with lullaby.*
Weaving spiders, come not here.

Act II Sc ii

A terrible mix-up

Demetrius, with Helena still following him, now arrives in this part of the wood but, in the darkness, he does not notice Hermia and Lysander asleep and he runs on. Helena, however, is tired and just as she decides to take a rest, she sees Lysander asleep and wakes him up. Because of the magic charm, he instantly falls in love with her – and to Helena's amazement, begins to declare his love with sweet words. Thinking that he is making fun of her, Helena becomes angry and leaves him in disgust – only to be followed by him. Hermia now wakes up from a bad dream and calls to Lysander but finds he has gone. Alarmed and afraid, she goes off in search of him.

Bottom turned into an ass

The rustic tradesmen now come into the wood to rehearse their play. By chance, they pick a spot close to where Titania lies asleep. As they talk about the play – Bottom is worried that the killings and lions in the story will upset the ladies – Puck comes upon them. Out of fun – for Puck is a naughty fellow – he decides to change Bottom into an ass. When his friends look up and see Bottom with the head of an ass, they become very alarmed and run away in fright. Bottom, unaware of how strange he looks, thinks he is being teased and that his friends are trying to frighten him.

Titania in love with an ass

Bottom sings a song to show how indifferent he is to being left alone but this awakens Titania. She immediately falls in love with him because of the magic flower that has been put in her eyes.

She leads him into her fairy bower and calls for her fairies, Pease Blossom, Cobweb, Moth, and Mustard Seed to attend to his every need.

In the meantime, Puck has returned to Oberon. He tells him that his trick has been successful – Titania has fallen in love with Bottom transformed into an ass and the young Athenian man has been given the love potion.

Demetrius has by this time found Hermia in the wood and he declares his love for her – but, as before, she refuses to accept him as a husband. Worried that some harm has come to Lysander, she goes off in search of him. Demetrius, by now exhausted, lets her go and he lies down to sleep.

19

> **Titania's instructions to her fairies**
> *Be kind and courteous to this gentleman;*
> *Hop in his walks, and gambol in his eyes;*
> *Feed him with apricocks and dewberries,*
> *With purple grapes, green figs, and mulberries.*
> *The honey bags steal from the humble-bees,*
> *And for night-tapers crop their waxen thighs,*
> *And light them at the fiery glow-worm's eyes,*
> *To have my love to bed-and to arise;*
> *And pluck the wings from painted butterflies*
> *To fan the moonbeams from his sleeping eyes:*
> *Nod to him, elves, and do him courtesies.*
>
> Act III Sc i

Oberon's plan to sort out the mix-up

Oberon and Puck now arrive in this part of the wood. Oberon recognizes Demetrius at once and realizes that Puck has mistakenly put the love potion in the eyes of the wrong young man. He at once sends Puck to find Helena and bring her back while he squeezes the magic juice into Demetrius's eyes. In that way when Demetrius wakes up he will – as Oberon intended in the first place – fall in love with Helena.

More complications

Puck is saved the trouble of searching for Helena because at that moment she and Lysander appear. Lysander declares his love for her but she is still upset and thinks he is making fun of her. Demetrius now wakes up and since Helena is the first thing he sees, he declares his love in the most glowing and lavish way. By now, Helena is very confused; she cannot understand why the two young men are in love with her, unless it is part of some joke they are playing just to humiliate her.

Hermia and Helena quarrel

Hermia now appears and is delighted at finding Lysander. When he swears that he is in love with Helena, Hermia thinks he is teasing. After a while she realizes he is not. To her astonishment, both men are now in love, not with her, but with her schoolfriend. She gets into a rage, thinking that Helena has deliberately turned Lysander against her and that all three are making fun of her in a hurtful way. Helena, confused and unable to understand it all, believes that Hermia's outburst is further proof that the three are plotting against her. This leads to a terrible quarrel between the two young women, in which they call each other names and even insult each other's appearance.

The two men also criticize Hermia and try to protect Helena from Hermia. Then they, too, begin to quarrel and go off into the forest to fight it out. Left alone with Hermia, Helena – who is timid by nature – decides to run away, rather than have her eyes scratched out by Hermia.

Oberon makes it better again

The quarrel has been watched by Oberon and Puck. Puck thinks it has all been great fun but Oberon is cross that his plans have gone awry – and he orders Puck to put things right. He is to keep the young men apart, leading each one astray until they are so exhausted that they fall asleep in separate parts of the forest. He is then to use another magic potion on Lysander which destroys the effect of the love flower. This means that when Lysander wakes up, he will be in love with Hermia – as he really was before.

By this time, too, Hermia and Helena have gone their separate ways but both are exhausted. All four lovers fall asleep in the wood. Unbeknownst to each other – because of the darkness – they are only a little distance apart.

21

Titania spellbound

Oberon in the meantime has gone off to find Titania to release her from the love spell. Bottom has been giving commands to the little fairies whom Titania has ordered to wait on him, but he becomes sleepy. Titania lovingly winds him in her arms and when Oberon arrives he finds this odd, ill-matched pair of lovers asleep. He uses a magic potion to release Titania from the love charm.

> **Titania with Bottom**
> *Come, sit upon this flow'ry bed,*
> *While I thy amiable cheeks do coy,*
> *And stick musk roses in thy sleek smooth head,*
> *And kiss thy fair large ears, my gentle joy.*
>
>
>
> Act IV Sc i

Oberon and Titania reconciled

Oberon tells Puck, who has joined him, that he has made up his quarrel with Titania. She has agreed that he can have the Indian boy as his page. When Titania wakes up, she tells Oberon of her dream. When he points to Bottom lying beside her, she is filled with horror and disgust. Oberon tells Puck to take off the ass's head from the sleeping Bottom and the fairies go off to prepare for the Duke's wedding.

What the hunters find

As dawn breaks on May 1, Theseus, Hippolyta, and members of the Athenian court set out from Athens on a hunting expedition. As they pass through the woods, they come upon the sleeping lovers. Thinking that they have arisen early to celebrate May 1, the Duke and his party wake them up.

23

Recounting the events of the midsummer night

Dazed and a little confused, the young lovers tell the Duke and Egeus, Hermia's father, about their reasons for being in the wood and the events of the past night. Demetrius, who is still under the magic spell, declares that he is really in love with Helena. His passion for Hermia was just a passing thing. Lysander, of course, has also found that his love for Hermia has returned. The Duke is pleased that the lovers' difficulties have been sorted out; and he declares that their weddings will be celebrated with his own. Although the lovers are still uncertain about whether or not they are in a dream, they all go off to Athens to prepare for the wedding celebrations.

Bottom wakes up

Bottom, alone in the forest, now wakes up. He is just as dazed as the lovers, with vague memories of the attentions of Titania and the fairies. He goes home and calls at Quince's house, to find that his friends have been concerned about him. But Bottom has heard that their play is to be performed before the Duke that night; and he orders everybody to go off and get ready for it.

The "tragedy" of Pyramus and Thisbe

The play is to be put on after the wedding ceremony and before the couples retire for the night. The Duke's master of ceremonies – who has seen the rustics rehearse – warns the Duke that the play is rather bad. The story of Pyramus and Thisbe is supposed to be a sad tale – but because the actors have never written or put on a play before, it turns out to be very funny. The tradesmen do not have any stage scenery, so they themselves act out not only the human characters but also other things that are in the play. These include a lion, a wall, the moon, and a lantern. This makes it

---

Theseus on the midsummer night's dream

I never may believe
These antique fables, nor these
*   fairy toys.*
Lovers and madmen have such
*   seething brains,*
Such shaping fantasies, that
*   apprehend*
More than cool reason ever
*   comprehends.*
The lunatic, the lover and the
*   poet*
Are of imagination all compact.
One sees more devils than vast
*   hell can hold,*
That is the madman. The lover,
*   all as frantic,*
Sees Helen's beauty in a brow of
*   Egypt.*
The poet's eye, in a fine frenzy
*   rolling,*
Doth glance from heaven to
*   earth, from earth to*
*   heaven;*
And as imagination bodies forth
The forms of things unknown, the
*   poet's pen*
Turns them to shapes, and gives
*   to airy nothing*
A local habitation and a name.

Act v Sc i

The fairies' blessing
Through the house give glimmering light,
By the dead and drowsy fire:
Every elf and fairy sprite
Hop as light as bird from brier;
And this ditty, after me,
Sing and dance it trippingly.

Act v Sc ii

even more amusing – although, of course, the tradesmen did not mean it to be comic. Happily, the newly married couples are very pleased with their entertainment.

The fairies' blessing

When the play is over and the night draws to a close, the actors and spectators go off to bed. Then the fairies come into the palace. They are there to bless the marriages and the house, which they do by singing and dancing. When Oberon and Titania leave, Puck remains. He explains that, to many people, the story of *A Midsummer Night's Dream* may seem silly. But he cheerfully apologizes and reminds us that dreams are often like that.

Puck's epilogue
If we shadows have offended,
Think but this, and all is mended:
That you have but slumber'd here,
While these visions did appear.
And this weak and idle theme,
No more yielding but a dream.

Act v Sc ii

The Play's Characters

Theseus and Hippolyta

Theseus on the craftsmen's play
> *I will hear that play;*
> *For never anything can be amiss,*
> *When simpleness and duty tender it.*

Act v Sc i

Theseus and Hippolyta
According to ancient Greek legend, Theseus was a great man who performed many brave deeds before he became ruler of Athens. Hippolyta, the lady whom he marries at the end of Shakespeare's play, was also a person of some importance, because she was the queen of a tribe of female warriors called the Amazons. According to ancient stories, Theseus went to war with the Amazons and after he had defeated them in battle he fell

in love with their queen. In the play, Theseus is a wise and sensible man and a good ruler. Although he is sorry for Hermia because she is in love with Lysander, he will not allow her to disobey the laws of Athens. Later in the play, he is the person who talks common sense when the lovers tell the story of their night in the woods. Although he is glad that their difficulties have been sorted out, he does not believe in dreams and fairy tales. These, he declares, only affect the brains of lovers and mad people. Real, everyday things are what he is concerned about.

He also shows that he is a kind man, and courteous and good-mannered to his subjects, as a good ruler should be. Theseus insists on seeing the Pyramus and Thisbe play. He knows that the humble folk have put a lot of effort into the play out of love and respect for their Duke. To Theseus, this is more important than whether the play is good or bad.

Hippolyta, too, is a fairly down-to-earth woman, She is fond of the open air and hunting and although she is a little puzzled by the midsummer night's events she, like Theseus, is glad that they have helped the lovers. Unlike her husband, she is bored by the play of Pyramus and Thisbe. "This is the silliest stuff that I ever heard," she says.

Oberon and Titania

Oberon and Titania are king and queen of a fairy kingdom and we know that they have come to the forest near Athens from India (where they seem to live most of the time) in order to bless the marriage of Theseus and Hippolyta.

Titania

Oberon

Because they are spirits, they have magical powers which, in this play, they use to help out the human beings. They are good fairies, unlike the witches in Shakespeare's play, *Macbeth*, who are evil. Oberon, for instance, uses the magic love juice to help the lovers

27

Helena on the nature of love

Things base and vile, holding no quantity,
Love can transpose to form and dignity.
Love looks not with the eyes, but with the mind,
And therefore is wing'd Cupid painted blind.

The young lovers

Shakespeare does not make Lysander and Demetrius, the two young Athenian men, really interesting people; he uses them more to show us what silly things people in love say and do. Demetrius is the more unkind of the two – he jilted Helena for Hermia and seems to care very little for poor Helena's feelings – while Lysander seems truly in love with Hermia, except when under the magic spell.

Shakespeare pays more attention to the young women. Helena is tall and fair and rather timid. For most of the play she is very unhappy because, although she is in love with Demetrius, he is not in love with her. She also does not have a great deal of confidence in herself.

Hermia is short, dark and quick-tempered. When she thinks Helena has stolen Lysander away from her, she is furious and threatens to scratch out Helena's eyes. When finally the lovers are awakened by Theseus, Demetrius, helped by the love juice, realizes he is in love with Helena and Lysander regains his love for Hermia. The lovers are now happy – and like Bottom, they remember the events of the night but they are not sure whether they were a dream or not.

Lysander and Hermia

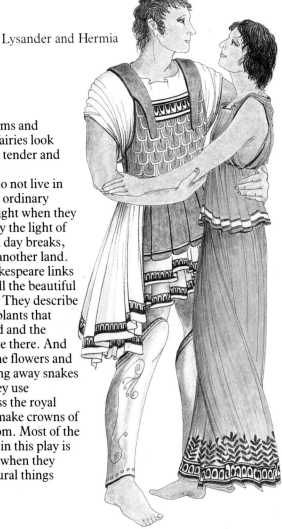

with their problems and Titania and her fairies look after Bottom in a tender and thoughtful way.

These fairies do not live in the daytime, like ordinary people, but by night when they dance and sing by the light of the moon. When day breaks, they fly away to another land. In this play, Shakespeare links the fairies with all the beautiful things of nature. They describe the flowers and plants that grow in the wood and the creatures that live there. And they look after the flowers and blossoms, keeping away snakes and spiders. They use dewdrops to bless the royal house and they make crowns of flowers for Bottom. Most of the beautiful poetry in this play is spoken by them when they describe the natural things around them.

Puck fetches the love potion

I'll put a girdle round about the earth
In forty minutes.

Act II Sci

Helena and Demetrius

Puck

Puck is a different kind of fairy from Oberon and Titania. Although he plays the part of Oberon's servant and messenger, he is more like the goblins that appeared in fairy stories when Shakespeare was a boy. In the play, he is also called Robin Goodfellow and Hobgoblin and this character was a mischievous fellow, well known in many fairy tales for the pranks he played.

One of Titania's fairies recognizes him as the goblin who makes fun of people and Puck himself describes the jokes he often plays on ordinary villagers. Sometimes he upsets the dairymaids by skimming the cream from the milk or by getting in the dairy churn so that they cannot turn the cream into butter. On other occasions, he spoils beer while it is being brewed, just for fun. Another favorite trick is to change himself into a crabapple hidden inside a jug of ale. Then, when an old grandmother sips the ale, he bobs against her lips so that she spills it. His best joke, however, is to whip away a stool from an old lady as she is talking so that when she falls flat on the floor, everyone laughs.

Although he is a mischievous goblin, Puck is good and kindhearted like the fairies. He goes

29

SHIRLEY STEINBERG

Puck

Bottom's instructions to the fairies
*. . . help Cavalery Cobweb to scratch. I must to the
barber's, mounsieur; for methinks I am marvellous
hairy about the face; and I am such a tender ass, if
my hair do but tickle me, I must scratch.*

Act IV Sci

Bottom

Shakespeare intended Bottom
and his fellow actors, the
tradesmen, to be comic
characters. They are funny,
rather like clowns. And we
laugh at them and their efforts
to put on their play.

Nick Bottom is a weaver and
he, along with his friends, is a
simple, uneducated man like
most of the ordinary citizens of
Athens. Although we laugh at
him, Bottom is a very likeable
person. He is so excited about the
play that he wants to play every part
himself, describing for us how he
would play each role in order to hold
the audience's attention. "Let me
play the lion, too," he says. "I will
roar, that I will do any man's heart
good to hear me."

Puck plays a trick on Bottom
by turning him into an ass and
Titania falls in love with him.

Bottom seems to be rather
amused by this and tells Titania
that she has little reason for
being in love with him. But he
decides to go along with her
infatuation and, like an actor in
a play, he jokes and chats with
Titania and the fairies, just as a
true gentleman would.

Bottom

ahead to clean the house before
the fairies bless it (in the fairy
stories of the time he often
helped with the housework)
and after they have flown away,
he stays behind to talk to the
people who have been
watching the play. Shakespeare
lets Puck explain to us that the
play is not meant to be very
serious but that it is rather like
a dream in which silly and
improbable things can happen.
If we have not enjoyed it, he
says, he will try to make up for
it with the next play we read or
see – which will be better.

30

SHIRLEY STEINBA

The Life and Plays of Shakespeare

Life of Shakespeare

1564 William Shakespeare born at Stratford-upon-Avon.

1582 Shakespeare marries Anne Hathaway, eight years his senior.

1583 Shakespeare's daughter, Susanna, is born.

1585 The twins, Hamnet and Judith, are born.

1587 Shakespeare goes to London.

1591-2 Shakespeare writes *The Comedy of Errors*. He is becoming well-known as an actor and writer.

1592 Theaters closed because of plague.

1593-4 Shakespeare writes *Titus Andronicus* and *The Taming of the Shrew*: he is member of the theatrical company, the Chamberlain's Men.

1594-5 Shakespeare writes *Romeo and Juliet*.

1595 Shakespeare writes *A Midsummer Night's Dream*.

1595-6 Shakespeare writes *Richard II*.

1596 Shakespeare's son, Hamnet, dies. He writes *King John* and *The Merchant of Venice*.

1597 Shakespeare buys New Place in Stratford.

1597-8 Shakespeare writes *Henry IV*.

1599 Shakespeare's theater company opens the Globe Theatre.

1599-1600 Shakespeare writes *As You Like It*, *Henry V*, and *Twelfth Night*.

1600-01 Shakespeare writes *Hamlet*.

1602-03 Shakespeare writes *All's Well That Ends Well*.

1603 Elizabeth I dies. James I becomes king. Theaters closed because of plague.

1603-04 Shakespeare writes *Othello*.

1605 Theaters closed because of plague.

1605-06 Shakespeare writes *Macbeth* and *King Lear*.

1606-07 Shakespeare writes *Antony and Cleopatra*.

1607 Susanna Shakespeare marries Dr. John Hall. Theaters closed because of plague.

1608 Shakespeare's granddaughter, Elizabeth Hall, is born.

1609 *Sonnets* published. Theaters closed because of plague.

1610 Theaters closed because of plague. Shakespeare gives up his London lodgings and retires to Stratford.

1611-12 Shakespeare writes *The Tempest*.

1613 Globe Theatre burns to the ground during a performance of Henry VIII.

1616 Shakespeare dies on April 23.

Shakespeare's plays

The Comedy of Errors
Love's Labour's Lost
Henry VI Part 2
Henry VI Part 3
Henry VI Part 1
Richard III
Titus Andronicus
The Taming of the Shrew
The Two Gentlemen of Verona
Romeo and Juliet
Richard II
A Midsummer Night's Dream
King John
The Merchant of Venice
Henry IV Part 1
Henry IV Part 2
Much Ado About Nothing
Henry V
Julius Caesar
As You Like It
Twelfth Night
Hamlet
The Merry Wives of Windsor
Troilus and Cressida
All's Well That Ends Well
Othello
Measure for Measure
King Lear
Macbeth
Antony and Cleopatra
Timon of Athens
Coriolanus
Pericles
Cymbeline
The Winter's Tale
The Tempest
Henry VIII

Index

Numerals in *italics* refer to picture captions.

Arden, Mary 4
As You Like It 7

Bottom 8, 14, 18, 19, 20, 22, 24, 28, 30
    character of 30
    his instructions to the fairies (quote) 30

Canterbury Tales, The 11
Charlecote Park 5
Chaucer, Geoffrey 11

dances 9, *9*, 10
Demetrius 9, 12, 14, 16, 17, 18, 19, 21, 24, 28
    character of 28
Drayton, Michael 6

Egeus 12, 24

fairies' blessing (quote) 25
    song (quote) 17
fairy tales 7, 11
fêtes and festivals 8, 10, 11
Flute 14

ghosts 8
    descriptions of (quote) 8

Hathaway, Anne 4, 7
Helena 9, 14, 16, 17, 18, 20, 21, 24, 28
    character of 28
    on the nature of love (quote) 28
Hermia 9, 12, 14, 16, 17, 18, 19, 20, 21, 24, 28
    character of 28
    description of (quote) 14
Hippolyta 9, 11, 12, 22, 26, 27
    character of 26
hunting 7, 14

Jonson, Ben 6

Lucy, Sir Thomas 5
Lysander 9, 12, 14, 16, 17, 18, 19, 20, 21, 24, 28
    character of 28

Macbeth 6, 7, 27

masques 10
May Day *8*, 11
midsummer night 10
Midsummer Night's Dream, A, story of 12-25
    Act I Scene 1 12
    Act I Scene 2 14
    Act II Scene 1 15
    Act II Scene 2 17
    Act III Scene 1 18
    Act III Scene 2 20
    Act IV Scene 1 22
    Act IV Scene 2 24
    Act V Scene 1 24
    Act V Scene 2 25
    Bottom turned into an ass 18
    Bottom wakes up 24
    the fairies' blessing 25
    Hermia and Helena quarrel 21
    how Helena betrays her friend 14
    the love potion 16
    lovers' difficulties 12
    more complications 20
    Oberon and Titania reconciled 22
    Oberon makes it better again 21
    Oberon's plan to sort out the mix up 20
    a plan to run away 12
    Puck's epilogue 25
    Puck's mistake 17
    quarrel of Oberon and Titania 15
    recounting the events of the
        midsummer night 24
    a royal wedding 12
    a terrible mix up 18
    Titania in love with an ass 18
    Titania spellbound 22
    the tradesmen and their play 14
    the "tragedy" of Pyramus and Thisbe 24
    what the hunters find 22

Oberon 15, 16, 17, 19, 20, 21, 22, 25, 27, 29
    character of 27

Puck 8, 15, 16, 17, 18, 20, 21, 22, 25, 29, 30
    character of 29
    his description of game birds (quote) 7
    his epilogue (quote) 225
    fetches the love potion (quote) 29
    his tricks (quote) 8

Quince 14, 24

Richard III 6
Romeo and Juliet 6

Shakespeare, Hamnet 4
    John 3
    Judith 4
    Susanna 4, 7
    William 3-8, 9, 10, 11, 27, 28, 30
Snug 14
Snout 14
songs 9, 10
Sonnets 5
    dark lady of 5
Southampton, Earl of 5, *5*
Starveling 14
Stratford-upon-Avon 3, *3*, 4, 5, *6*, 7, 8

Taming of the Shrew, The 6
Theseus 6, 9, 11, 12, 14, 15, 22, 24, 26, 27
    character of 26
    on the craftsmen's play (quote) 26
    his hounds (quote) 6
    on the midsummer night's dream
        (quote) 24
Titania 15, 17, 18, 19, 20, 22, 24, 25, 27, 28, 30
    character of 27
    instructions to her fairies (quote) 20
    where she sleeps (quote) 16
    with Bottom (quote) 22
Twelfth Night 10

wedding celebrations 9, 11
What You Will 10

Acknowledgments
The publishers would like to thank Morag Gibson for her help in producing this book.

Picture credits
p.1 Governors of Royal Shakespeare Theatre, p.5 National Portrait Gallery (reproduction courtesy Lady Anne Bentinck), p.11 John R. Freeman (reproduction courtesy The Marquess of Salisbury).

SHIRLEY STEINBACH